PRAISE FOR GORMAN POETRY

"The poems have an addictive quality, and I found myself reading them again and again, as the deceptively simple words made me feel calm, peaceful and contemplative ... They speak to the soul. Highly recommended."
—Llewelyn author, *Richard Webster*

"I am enchanted by the ease with which the poet manages to talk about complex topics in a simple and clear way. I have not found many books comparable. Gorman has a knack for touching the heart of a sensitive reader. He also has a delicate and honest way of writing, and I believe this is what makes the collection valuable."
—*Astrid Iustulin*

"Well-chosen words convey all that is beautiful ... and true about the human condition. They convey emotionality without being emotional, love without being sappy, and insight without being preachy. *The Lightness of Being* is rich with words that connote wisdom from years lived, mistakes made, and a life embraced. This is a body of work that's evocative and invites his audience to let the words take them on a spiritual journey that's impossible to resist."
—*Marta Tandori*

OTHER WORKS BY THIS AUTHOR

*Poems of Life, Love,
and the Meaning of Meaning*

Poet Gone Wild

Sojourn

THE LIGHTNESS OF BEING

GORMAN POETRY

Copyright © 2022, 2024 Paul J. Gorman
All Rights Reserved

Year of the Book
135 Glen Avenue
Glen Rock, PA 17327

ISBN: 978-1-64649-420-0 (paperback)
ISBN: 978-1-64649-421-7 (ebook)

Cover photo: Taken in Western Maryland by the author.

No part of this publication may be reproduced, distributed, or transmitted in any form or by any means, including photocopying, recording, or other electronic or mechanical methods, without the prior written permission of the author, except in the case of brief quotations embodied in critical reviews and certain other noncommercial uses permitted by copyright law.

DISCLAIMER: The poems in this book may cause feelings of ease, upliftment, and true healing—and are solely the manifestation of the reader.

Contents

Customer Service 1
We Can Be 4
You'll Love When You See 6
Meaning That Lives 10
Heart of Godness 12
All But Me 16
Always One In My Eyes 18
It Depends What You See 21
Forgive and Forget 22
What Will Surely Be 24
More Than What Is 26
I Googled God 30
I Believe 32
You'll See Only Me 34
A Bull Recalls His Time In A China Shop 38
The Joke Is On Me 40
You Will Not Be Alone 43
Your Gift 46
Saints and Sages 48
Pleasant Surprises 50
100% 52

Only One You 55
The List (All That There Is) 57
Love is Me 60
All Is Forgiven 64
Our Saving Grace 67
I'm Not Keeping Score 69
Only As We... 72
One and One Makes You..................................... 75
I'll Love Being You 78
I AM Me.. 80
My Moment With You... 82
Now They Are Light 85
C+.. 87

CUSTOMER SERVICE

The checkout clerk
   had asked if I got
all I was looking for
    and I said I had not

do you sell a strawberry
    heart repair
sweet peace in a can
    or a smile I can wear

and corrective glasses
    to make memories fair
and heal old wounds
    I need a pair

I could have gone on
    but saw in his stare
I was not ready for checkout
    and he pointed to where

I saw Customer Service
    and God was there
ready to help me
    and make me aware

Feel free to sit down
    there appeared a chair
life is change
    which can create despair

it's easy to think
    that I don't care
and life is hard
    or it isn't fair

but change is good
    always in the air
to create what you want
    and make more to share

I am all and you
    so we won't compare
choosing love in each moment
    will be our prayer

So how could it be
    that God would appear
at Customer Service
    Employee of the Year?

You had asked for help
    I heard in my ear
when choosing love
    it brings you near

love is sincere
    God without fear
fear interferes
    now it is clear

Then let me ask you
    while I am here
what am I afraid of
    even afraid to hear?

That you could fail
    will be alone
or judged by others
    with nothing to own

it either isn't possible
    or is not true
doesn't matter
    or is not for you

when you choose love
    in whatever you do
loving life and yourself
    you choose me too

WE CAN BE

I had confided
    in God last night
that I don't know Godness
    except in what's right

and even so
    it's subject to change
just a matter of opinion
    in our domain

based on perception
    through our beliefs
the Godness inception
    created in peace

or in a big bang
    a violent release
an immaculate conception
    the wonders won't cease

so let me know
    and let it rhyme
please tell me the story
    the beginning of time

I wanted to see
    what you would do
given a surprise
    the mystery of you

would you love it
    or send it back
not even see it
    or need to attack

your own creation
    not subject to lack
your mental projection
    as a matter of fact

that was the best
    that I could give
your freedom to act
    and a will to live

Thanks so much!
    a universal gift
one size fits all
    I love what you did

or was it done by me
    a projection to see
and to know the Godness
    that we can be

You'll Love When You See

The universe responds
    to nothing else
but the way I feel
    about myself

do I feel neglected
    affected and rejected
or do I feel loved
    accepted and protected

and not just loved
    in a receiving role
but being the love
    and I am the Whole

pretty amazing
    that the universe could be
an extension of feelings
    only coming from me

so I flow the source
    through a prism of feelings
my life creation
    made real for self-healing

let's go inside
    to examine this
where there's only peace
    and all time exists

what does it prove
    what does it need
infinite energy
    to be coming through me?

It wants to feel
    and it wants to do
its own magnificence
    as me and you

Does it really need me
    can't it just be
does it need mixed feelings
    that don't agree?

maybe that's it
    and what it asks of me
is to love myself
    and love I will see

a little tricky
    now I feel apart
let's try again
    and each moment I start

I am compassion
    so will not get mad
I have no fear
    but can still be sad

I am complete
    love comes from within
all time and creation
    about to begin

does that make sense
    that life starts here
there is no offense
    to create anger or fear?

then you haven't seen
    my daily commute
reckless drivers that speed
    all along my route

you should see at work
    the laziness and greed
and on the computer
    deception and need

or in the news
    playing violent feeds
our Garden of Eden
    growing lots of weeds

This week it will change
    when you stand in your power
you'll love when you see
    each weed is a flower

Meaning that Lives

What's the point
   of being alive
what's the purpose
   why even try?

where's the meaning
   in trying to survive
knowing I'm leaving
   but not why I arrived

You came to be
   and you came to do
free to see
   what you can improve

or to destroy
   and create anew
or not see at all
   if you so choose

it happens a lot
  you'll see in the news
how people forgot
  or simply refuse

to honor life
  and each other's views
or respect themselves
  by speaking the truth

so consider this
  that the meaning is
by loving yourself
  you're loving what is

to heal in time
  love receives and gives
you are my divine
  meaning that lives

Heart of Godness

I had no self-worth
   right after my birth
not that I can recall
   that or anything at all

no goals or ambition
   no confidence or fear
born in transition
   still in my first year

my greatest achievement
   besides getting here
was being greeted by love
   dear hearts beating near

That's what you know
   because that's what you are
coming from Oneness
   and born with one heart

beating a rhythm
   measures in time
one after the other
   One heartbeat in mine

you came to be
　to see what to see
looking for love
　because you came from me

you were also taught
　that I wouldn't agree
and with that thought
　you couldn't be free

Unless I forgive
　myself and others
I'd rather not
　if I had my druthers

That is fine
　but only hurts you
which isn't possible
　from our Oneness view

except in your mind
　where you crash and burn
and find separation
　or refuse to learn

mad at yourself
　not allowed to be free
looking around
　there is only me

which also includes you
   a Oneness of we
the Heart of Godness
   feeling healed to be

Well, I don't doubt
   that you mean well
with spiritual talk
   in our living hell

what is the point
   of our being here
non-love all around
   in what I see and hear?

Now you have it
   and what I want to make clear
how you feel about yourself
   is where you heal your fear

that is projected out
   finding separate divisions
something to fight
   in your grand Inquisitions

yes, it's hell
   and it won't go away
crashing and burning
   day after day

until you make up your mind
*   that the fight is within*
conflicted in Oneness
*   is as silly as sin*

or should I say guilty
*   now there's a sore topic*
and rightfully so
*   until you choose to stop it*

which is why you came
*   to try again*
and enlighten yourself
*   to lessen the pain*

you think you left Godness
*   not possible or true*
the physical illusion
*   is only coming from you*

we're making good progress
*   and what I suggest that you do*
is to forgive yourself
*   for believing it's true*

in your own creation
*   each moment is new*
hearts beating our Oneness
*   Heart of Godness is in you*

All But Me

I need to know
   what I'm doing here
*Counting your blessings
   and facing your fears*

Maybe we could meet
   over a couple of beers
on me, of course
   just to be clear

*Yes, let's meet
   I am all ears
ALL as in all ways
   so I will always hear*

*I am all
   but there is all I am not
your fears and regrets
   until you healed and forgot*

and then there is doubt
  guilt and shame used a lot
used as in useful
  until they were not

but they came from you
  and could not be from me
you set up the contrast
  to easily see

that which is real
  and will always be
and what is a dream
  that is all but me

(now let's count your blessings
  while we wait for our beers
if we list them all
  we'll be counting for years)

[the bartender was nice
  "Are you expecting a friend?
I'll keep one on ice,
  just let me know when."]

Always One In My Eyes

The problem with the past
   the way it's received
is not what I did
   but in the way it's perceived

through a harsher lens
   of right and wrong
what's good and bad
   weak and strong

which makes it worse
   and a bigger regret
into an unfair curse
   that's hard to forget

What you would see
   if you were me
is that your judgment
   is ill conceived

to see your mistakes
*   that you want to review*
but keep raising the stakes
*   to continually improve*

maybe each life
*   should start in reverse*
innocence is last
*   and wisdom is first*

which way would you go
*   if you had to choose*
wisdom with a past
*   and would innocence lose?*

to tell you the truth
*   that couldn't be*
you can only be both
*   innocent and free*

you are wiser now
*   but self-deceived*
and you want to know how
*   you can be relieved*

of guilt and regret
*   for what has gone before*
it seemed right at the time
*   or you chose to ignore*

now you've paid the price

*actually paid more
for what wisdom costs
what is wisdom for?*

*an enlightened mind
and expanded awareness
through all lines in time
and in all fairness*

*you are doing just fine
but what you never knew
self-love is forgiveness
that is gifted by you*

*though in our illusion
guilt isn't real
only Oneness is love
or else it's to heal*

*so now you are both
innocent and wise
from all that you chose
always One in my eyes*

*(but it's up to you
and when you decide
that you are One too
One love that's inside)*

It Depends What You See

Some spiritual texts
say evil doesn't exist
there is only love
   or a lack of this

and lack is a perception
   a mental deception
it was not created
   or a part of conception

What you see
   is what you get
a feedback loop
   that's always set

by your intention
   and love attention
the clever part
   of our invention

is that it begins with you
   and ends with me
or the other way around
   it depends what you see

FORGIVE AND FORGET

Where can I find
   peace of mind
and have it now
   to carry through time

and what would it mean
   to have this peace
with fear and worry
   and doubts released?

by my own thoughts
   reflecting in ease
a memory loss
   is more what I need

What you can do
   is learn to forgive
beginning with you
   and you can begin to live

then forgive the rest
   it was only a game
to see the purpose
   of why they came

into your creation
    with the power you use
it's in your thoughts
    where there's power to choose

how to respond or react
    which makes how you feel
when you interact
    it creates how you heal

not the acts of others
    they own their own minds
you only own yourself
    so to yourself be kind

the bottom line
    is to know your perception
and what needs forgiving
    is your self-deception

a good memory loss
    is one of regrets
your own perfect flaws
    you can forgive and forget

What Will Surely Be

The tiniest atoms
   that we cannot see
how could it be
   that they would agree

to form into elements
   one hundred and eighteen
making molecules and cells
   then into organs and me

forming animals and plants
   the earth and seas
the entire cosmos
   to infinite degrees

Let's back up
   to where you said 'me'
to find love in the order
   and what do you see?

there's only one place
   where balance breaks down
but it forms your reality
   and it's only found

in your thoughts
　　and in your beliefs
in fear and doubts
　　or in love and peace

what powers your atoms
　　each creative and free
the love of Godness
　　your power is me

(and in this moment
　　when we always meet
is where atoms create
　　what will surely be)

More Than What Is

What I need
   is goodness and peace
so how can I find
   both of these

I've seen examples
   of what they can be
but no longer believe
   that they come only from me

maybe they do
   or don't even exist
at least not in abundance
   and there is no bliss

Now there's a puzzle
   and you have something to do
to find more pieces
   that bring peace to you

I like dogs
   flowers and poems
to see the birds
   and to be at home

quite a bore
   I already know
but I like to explore
   the realm of unknown

let's cut to the chase
   tell me some more
what is reality
   what is it for?

I'm tired of anger
   bitterness and hate
don't tell me about fear
   or what I create

not while I'm here
   marooned out in space
with villains and goons
   always in my face

at least in the news
   what a disgrace
humanity is doomed
   and picking up the pace

That's their world view
   they have film crews to make
enough to confuse
   the whole human race

it's not about them
it's only about you
and the way that you feel
in each moment that's new

do you feel excited
to have one more chance
another day in your life
to see your soul advance?

remember again
what you like to see
the love of dogs
and birds and flowers being free

see what they teach
and what you said you need
exploring love and peace
and how you reached me

expanding my Oneness
beyond All That Is
like poems out of nothing
is why creation exists

All becomes more
you're inflating What Is
not at all a bore
you're making great bliss

here's a contradiction
   the news won't report
if there's All That Is
   how could there be more?

the universe expands
   in only one direction
and when I say in
   I mean introspection

look inside
   as you've been meaning to do
and when I say meaning
   means it's meant for you

so you are the receiver
   creating goodness that lives
with peace in each moment
   you're now More Than What Is

(and another clue
   that you can use
is that your goodness and peace
   others could use too)

I Googled God

I googled God
and they had his picture
did I say 'His'
   the same as in scripture

kind of old
   up in a cloud
lack of oxygen
   created a shroud

Quite a mystery
   my appearance
always here
   in a sheer coherence

being the opposite
   of whatever you fear
and forever near
   with no interference

I like to hear
   of your adherence
only to love
   and of fear's disappearance

*that's what I look like
   or how I appear to you
and you'll look like me
   when you are love too*

*so to google God
   just look in a mirror
I am still clear
   and you will see me clearer*

I Believe

I don't believe
   I'm just sayin'
but I'd like to relieve
    some thoughts I've been prayin'

to some degree
    nothing is free
and if I have to believe
    I will believe in me

I don't believe either
    so I'm with you
since there's only love
    only love will do

you prayed for strength
    and I gave you courage
to hold onto your vision
    and not be discouraged

you prayed for truth
  and got spiritual eyes
to see to the root
  behind all the lies

I'm just sayin'
  the answer is 'yes'
to what you've been prayin'
  and to your requests

the only thing
  you had asked of me
was for strength and truth
  you were ready to receive

it was always there
  inside of your heart
where you can truly feel
  we are not apart

talk about truth
  and the courage to see
that you're One with me
  then I believe we agree

You'll See Only Me

Could my personal life
  be an epic fail
with life as a hammer
  and me as a nail?

that's not really right
  because I'm doing just fine
but some hopes and dreams
  had a really hard time

was I not deserving
  if I look within
at least once in a while
  to bring in a win?

so then why not
  or should I say why
sabotage my own dreams
  and see that they die?

I hammered away
  until my wishes were killed
and in self-defeat
  I became quite skilled

and why was that
   when is enough enough
the only hammer
   could be a lack of love

love was there
   it would come and go
but it was up to me
   to open the flow

flowing to myself
   so that life could show
that from my heart
   every dream would grow

I will use the tools
   to reap what I sow
and if I sow only love
   then only love I will know

That sounds very good
   and is also true
but it doesn't explain
   what happens to you

if you still think
   that you have failed
and had also said
   that you were nailed

those are your words
  in a harsh description
usually reserved
  for a crucifixion

are you a victim
  of what you believe?
the whole depiction
  is what you conceived

come down from your cross
  there is no need
to punish yourself
  when you think like me

how can you do that?
  you just need to ask
and my holy spirit
  fulfills the task

I am like water
  poured into a flask
taking its shape
  however it's cast

uplift your thoughts
  spirit helps you to see
I am guiding your life
  and providing the leads

for our way to be
 to heal and be free
if you see only love
 you'll see only me

[and I'll tell you this
 so you stop regressing
those epic fails
 were actually blessings

spirit was busy
 thwarting your self-destruction
and didn't get a break
 from your mental constructions

when giving us thanks
 for saving the day
think hazardous duty
 deserves extra pay]

A Bull Recalls His Time in a China Shop

Walls and ceilings
  boundaries and feelings
delicate displays
  customers reeling

damaged and destroyed
  more than a mess
destruction employed
  to make do with less

who let him in
  an uninvited guest
they can begin healing
  with more room I guess

I'll tell you this
  one bull to another
the gentle approach
  is the way to work wonders

destruction is fine
  and needed sometimes
but in your own mind
  and dealing with lies

arranged on shelves
  for selected times
glass and porcelain
  this one is mine

oops, it fell
  right on the floor
what used to sell well
  has value no more

let's pick up the truth
  trampled and gored
it will never break
  here's what it's for

to guide you in life
  it's me at your core
see it shine in the light
  the shop is restored

The Joke Is On Me

How many times
   can one heart beat
did I say beat
   I meant to say break

and how much time
   can one heart ache
did I say ache
   I meant to say take

can it make a mistake
   and not admit defeat
why does it feel
   that it cannot be free

It did not break
   but was only bruised
and it did not heal
   because you refused

to see the truth
   in your reviews
of all the times
   you did not choose

love and peace
 and goodness would lose
if you could see me
 you'd see I'm amused

because when you go back
 and think about then
do you think about you
 or think about them?

my, oh my
 were they offended
and couldn't take a joke
 at least not as intended

let's send them a blessing
 when the thoughts appear
and stop distressing
 it's not what you fear

they forgave you
 as you forgave them
feeling it now
 is healing it when

the joke is on you
 because in the end
in a cosmic sense
 I will mend

all that was said
 and all that was done
there's no defense
 when the truth has won

so you'll have to laugh
 and I think you'll agree
if All is one
 then the joke is on me

(did I say laugh
 I should have said "gaffe"
Ha! there I go again
 gaffes from the past!)

You Will Not Be Alone

I believe in God
   actually that's all there is
everything else
   is an illusion that lives

in my mind
   that perceives and forgives
just to know the love
   it receives and gives

I don't golf at all
   but if I did
I'd keep my eye on the ball
   I learned as a kid

to advance down the field
   and take my time
with challenges revealed
   that they are only mine
when the game is over

I will find
that the illusion seemed real
   and was all in my mind

designed to heal
   time to feel and be kind
that was my deal
   several strokes behind

There is no score
   you have always won
please pardon my pun
   but you made a Whole in One

the challenges were fun
   you can play again
we'll meet in the clubhouse
   and I'll see you when

your game is done
   earning a rest to restore
from our days in the sun
   and to learn what they're for

advancing in the field
   you said it before
to improve and be healed
   since you designed the course

to tell you the truth
  you'll heal just the same
keep your eye on the ball
  it is only your game

talk about Oneness
  and being on your own
even out in the rough
  you will not be alone

Your Gift

It's clear to me
   each person is unique
and signed up for life
   where they wanted to be

to discover their gifts
   always God-given
and to share them with others
   openly or hidden

and also to learn
   how to discern
some gifts are endowed
   and others are earned

You will always receive
   what you have allowed
and in what you believe
   which brings me to how

the only wealth
  is in what you give away
and the way to health
  is in what you say

to yourself
  and to me in a way
that you're glad you received
  my gifts to display

by celebrating life
  from day to day
and in what you achieve
  come what may

adding love to life
  and love to your soul
which gifts back to me
  making us whole

[thank you for sharing
  you gave me a lift
and all of life
  has received your gift]

SAINTS AND SAGES

If the saints and sages
   all agree on one thing
it's that God is love
   as the love we bring

in peace and harmony
   love and light
it's why the birds sing
   and why there is life

flowing in time
   through a physical existence
into our hearts and minds
   at an imagined distance

I used to say
   you can't get there from here
but you can feel apart
   if you follow a fear

To be more precise
  you cannot go there
there is only here
  and here is where

there is only love
  harmony and peace
follow your heart
  and prepare to release

fear and needs
  and if you can believe
what saints and sages could see
  there's only here with me

go as far as you want
  you are never alone
and know that all roads
  will only lead you to home

Pleasant Surprises

There is no death
   just a really cool dream
and there's not much left
   for the fool I've been

who was I
   to want the best
for every creature
   more or less

what was I thinking
   wanting truth to prevail
and if that's true
   how could it fail?

who am I to try
   to judge or deny
I know that I'm here
   but the question is 'why?'

I've shown you before
   and I'll tell you again
you've come to explore
   and now is when

you creatively express
  and manifest what you need
to do your best
  in word and in deed

I have to confess
  that you had agreed
and what I profess
  is planting the seed

life can be short
  long enough to see
and as your last resort
  you will come to me

because in the end
  if there is such a thing
love cannot send
  and love cannot bring

there's no place to go
  just one place of being
and no death you could know
  as love flowing a dream

(in your dream I'll appear
  in infinite disguises
where there is no fear
  as pleasant surprises)

100%

I will lose
  one hundred percent
my life and money
  and on which they were spent

how can I detach
  from a loser's role
maybe in death
  I will be made whole

or maybe I won't
  and I just forgot
that I had never lost
  or received what I got

that I was always one
  things came and went
and one is a lot
  in one hundred percent

Only one is real
  the rest was to heal
to pretend you're apart
  then see how you feel

do you feel alright?
  we can make more time
to stay and fight
  or be a light to shine

and shine on what?
  your present decision
that one hundred percent
  is complete in division

there is your answer
  and I know you will find
that you are not your body
  but a mind in mine

you will also let go
  of all that you dreamed
and then you will know
  life is not what it seemed

I think I can see
  and I know what you mean
that there is only love
  and it's not always seen

but it is up to me
    and to my intent
to see only love
    one hundred percent

That's all you need
    you are One in me
and we are a team
    and free to be

your life is meant
    to heal what you dreamt
to know only love is
    one hundred percent

ONLY ONE YOU

What is the meaning
 behind my purpose
and why am I dreaming
 this three-ring circus?

To see what you are
 and what you are being
first see what you're not
 and where love is agreeing

then you will feel
 the whole expanding
right into you
 for your soul understanding

Why would I want
 to see what I'm not
then see all as One
 I knew, but forgot

I am the love
  and so are you
but only as One
  although it seems like two

healing flawed beliefs
  opposing energies release
creating more light
  to infinitely increase

making your world
  with the truth that you use
the cosmos is designed
  for you to choose

from multiple views
  as you decide
what's true inside
  where I am your guide

being only One
  and all that One includes
life has two sides
  for only One you

(illusion is side two)

The List (All That There Is)

There are some things
   that don't really exist
outside of me
   and here is a list

love and peace
   all happiness
only those three
   unless I have missed

the Oneness of God
   and eternal bliss
inside I will see
   they are all there is

who am I kidding
   to consider this
and is the source of pain
   what I resist?

You can only be

what's on your list
if you want to be free
inside I'll assist

you had said 'source'
and source only knows
love of course
and love only flows

in outward directions
flowing through your core
without any force
what is it for?

as you will allow
my peace always lives
and you are how
my love only gives

it's all that exists
and all that can be
what's on your list
All that is me

(so to be outside
it has to come from you
all from inside
for you to choose

just to be clear
  it's what you can use
if it's not on your list
  then you could lose

and chase illusions
  make mistakes in confusion
and only create
  without inclusion

of what you want
  and what you love
created in peace
  as listed above

so my suggestion
  is to choose from your list
and your selection will be
  All that there is)

Love Is Me

The world doesn't need
   my advice or support
my considered opinion
   or a status report

it doesn't want
   what I think and know
and what I forgot
   or need to let go

it doesn't care
   about how I feel
or if I'm not well
   and trying to heal

or maybe it does
   and provides healing for free
sharing its secrets
   for its life to see

I should have thanked it
   for all of the above
its support and knowing
   with healing and love

it always provides
    all that we need
an abundance of wellness
    that we eat and breathe

grounded in wisdom
    the land and the seas
in all of creation
    how could this be?

on top of that
    along comes me
thinking I'm right
    believing I'm free

Yes, right you are
    when in your right mind
and free to believe
    to love and to find

more of the same
    love's infinite supply
you had asked me how
    but the question is why

because that is me
    and so are you
and only as love
    we can be and do

*that's what is real
    and makes life renew
so I will tell you
    in a verse or two*

*life is temporary
    and passes away
and so does the sadness
    but the love always stays*

*that is why
    and what you will find
you are made for love
    from the love of mine*

Why again?

*To know only love
    is to know nothing less,
then you can express
    only love at its best*

*you will always be
    as you look you will see
you had asked me why
    and said 'along comes me'*

that's really it
*   and here's a suggestion*
you can be the answer
*   instead of the question*

there are only three words
*   you can ever be*
every question's answer is
*   'Love is me'*

that's what the world needs

ALL IS FORGIVEN

I love myself
despite my flaws
and I'll never be perfect
   I know because

if I was
   I would have to pause
and forgive myself
   make it my cause

If I could jump in
   I would like to say
that it's not so hard
   there's an easier way

first you acknowledge
   allow and accept
that you were learning to live
   when not very adept

at seeing signs
   or hearing my voice
life is designed
   as a matter of choice

so overall
*   you made some good moves*
and then moved on
*   when you would lose*

what else could you do
*   there's nothing to prove*
but to be true to you
*   as you improve*

as I was explaining
*   what needs to heal*
there are flaws remaining
*   in the way that you feel*

shame and guilt
*   from a past of living*
your future is built
*   when at last forgiving*

you meant no harm
*   but are hurting yourself*
with weapons and arms
*   turned toward your health*

all is forgiven
*   you wouldn't do it again*
or use the same words
*   to convey what you meant*

let me repeat
  because now is when
all is forgiven
  for what happened then

which is now in my heart
  healed and cleared
I only know love
  so don't know what you feared

let's move on
  together as one
you can now love yourself
  our flaws are gone

(time is for healing
  in an endless run
all is forgiven
  just ask and it's done)

OUR SAVING GRACE

I tried to forgive
myself and forget
but my self declined
   and refused to accept

what came up
   that's permanently saved
and what went down
   how I behaved

pushing the limits
   of social norms
now pushing back
   reformed to conform

Consider this
   what a social norm is
you say you're sorry
   and the other forgives

it works both ways
   so both can live
you and your past
   parents and kids

to your present self
　　your past could say
please forgive me
　　I am willing to change

then what happens
　　in forgiving mistakes
is that all of life heals
　　for goodness sakes

your self-correcting
　　is your conscience and guide
what better choice
　　than for you to decide

what is best
　　and what to teach correctly
what needs to heal
　　and to feel directly

is love through time
　　our healing place
the love of mine
　　our saving grace

I'M NOT KEEPING SCORE

There's not much in it
  for me anymore
just more disappointments
  and I'm not keeping score

Yes, you are
  and you're totally sure
that all of your hopes
  are worth hoping for

you had hoped for peace
  and the love which you feel
both timeless and real
  to be eternally healed

you can hope and love
  and look for wonder too
but where that lives
  is inside of you

that's my secret
  and all you will need
if you work with these
  you will be working with me

creating from your core
* to open new doors*
I'm not keeping score
* but we'll keep making more*

from love and peace
* they will increase*
surrounding your dreams
* as they heal into me*

which makes more light
* opening windows in time*
every thought and choice
* will start to align*

your heart and mind
* how life was designed*
always in motion
* for you to find*

and light your way back
* not an easy climb*
where thoughts can attack
* and hide my shine*

allow them to go
* and love their release*
then you will know
* how to make peace*

Yeah, well
  I guess you could say
if it's not loving or healed
  then it would be fake

It's fake in a sense
  that it only exists
to be forgiven and healed
  or it will persist

to only make more
  not what you wished
disappointments galore
  and only more of this

feel your love shine
  peace in all directions
and bless the divine
  in its wonderful perfection

by loving what is
  you're the healing ointment
there is no 'dis'
  in life's appointment

scheduled in time
  you're doing just fine
as the healer assigned
  to light the worlds of mine

ONLY AS WE

I'm still disappointed
and feel disjointed
like I was appointed
as a fly in the ointment

talking to Oneness
is all very good
but out here in the field
it's less understood

that we choose with our minds
and create with our hearts
through all lines in time
that are opened in part

for us to heal
so God is revealed
and together we feel
only love can be real

when unconcealed
that was our deal
right from the source
which is us, of course

I'd like to suggest
  just as a test
and even insist
  for you to do this

try being two
  and what would you do
if you were like me
  and not the One you?

*You just answered
  your very own question
and I've taken you up
  on your suggestion*

*we are always one
  believing we're two
but as one of each
  unique in each view*

*now I'd like to suggest
  just as a test
and even insist
  for you to do this*

*imagine you're me
  and what you would do
as my twoness to see
  how Oneness could be*

Well, I don't know
  if I agree with you
when I look around
  and see more than two

and I'm quite disturbed
  to tell you the truth
you've probably heard
  and I can give you proof

that life is a mass
  of contradictions
and in time will pass
  with my convictions

Again you answered
  your very own question
all will pass
  and you'll retain the lesson

that there is only love
  and only one me
and only as you
  we can only be

only as we

ONE AND ONE MAKES YOU

*Begin by forgiving
yourself and others
since both are one
   you'll forgive one another*

*and by loving yourself
   which also includes them
but starts with you
   so now is when*

*you power creation
   from inside your heart
the eternal cycle
   that requires a spark*

*subatomic reactions
   lighting within
to create your world
   the universe begins*

*to rock your world
   projecting it new
the one thing that's real
   love directed from you*

Why does it seem
    that hope disappears
if life is a dream
    and why are there fears?

Fear is a sign
    that your connection is low
and you're willing to believe
    what I'll never know

there is only love
    the energy of creation
flowing through you
    and your imagination

making your life
    and all that unfolds
out of my control
    or so I am told

your life is a dream
    and I have no doubt
that it seems very real
    but won't heal without

love flowing through
    what you see and do
a collaborative effort
    between me and you

to think we're apart
  in a world gone mad
with both light and dark
  good and bad

at least in your dream
  that you believe to be true
what you have conceived
  I've agreed to it too

some people say
  one and one makes two
but if I'm One and love
  then one and one makes you

I'll Love Being You

Is the purpose of life
   to discern truth from illusion
the wheat from the chaff
   wisdom from confusion?

talk about endless
   and I'm not keeping score
but if lies had value
   we'd never be poor

What are lies
   and what are they for?
you can lie to yourself
   and nothing more

close your eyes
   and use me as your guide
the truth all lies
   inside at your core

so let me ask you
  if the lies are disguised
or can you see the love
  can you gladly try?

and if you do
  it's where I come through
you'll be what you see
  and I'll love being you

I Am Me

Fear of losing
   fear of winning
the root of all evil
   has fear at the beginning

and losing what?
   money and status
prestige and appearance
   esteem apparatus

or to lose it all
   life and limb
does it count as a loss
   if I'm afraid to win?

and winning what?
   what is to gain?
just more protection
   to avoid any pain

I can also learn
   why we came
to grow in awareness
   to know and to change

and change to what?
   why and what for?
Infinite and fearless
   when less is more

to be only love
   or to eternally try
until we are One
   and that is why

That all sounds fine
   I appreciate the reply
but if we are One
   then who am I?

You are my savior
   and you help me to see
that if I could change
   you are how I would be

always loving
   and only love I would see
being One with you
   I Am glad I Am me

My Moment With You

What will be here
   in a thousand years
will the sun still shine
   to dry all the tears?

will there still be rain
   to wash away the pain?
will the earth remain
   with nothing to gain?

will the seasons renew
   the way that they do
except for the fears
   left by me and you?

how would it be
   with no imbalance or strife
could the earth go on
   without us in life?

maybe so, well
   definitely yes
the life that is gone
   will be us I guess

why can't we
    just live in peace
and appreciate life
    to let love increase?

You said the key words
    'love and peace'
'renew and you'
    those are the keys

to survive and thrive
    and I'll tell you why
to know the joy
    of being alive

and it doesn't matter
    where or when
you will grow in awareness
    now or then

Are you trying to say
    that the life we know
will be gone one day
    with nothing to show?

Every day ends
    to start over anew
except for one thing
    love coming from you

that lives forever
   in my eternal mind
the love I could never
   hope to find

so I chose you
   to create what I could
my co-creator
   of love and good

but you should know
   in my eternal view
there's no thousand years
   just my moment with you

[or should I say
   'as you' or 'for you'
there's no time at all
   after or before you]

Now They Are Light

I confess
  I was not at my best
the dozens of times
  when I failed the test

and went out of my lane
  out of my league
no one to blame
  only me

maybe the poem
  should end right here
along with the shame
  the same every year

What you can do
  to be truly healed
is to take your regrets
  how you truly feel

roll them up tight
  shrink-wrapped and sealed
hold them in the light
  no need to kneel

You can have them
  just let me know
I've added a label
  they are ready to go

I will recycle
  transmute and shift
repurpose and repackage
  what you have shipped

they were kind of heavy
  but that's alright
I have healed them with love
  now they are light

C+

You would think
   I'm not afraid to fail
I've had enough practice
   left a steady trail

of poor judgment
   missteps and errors
regrettable mistakes
   now memorable terrors

Think of life
   as learning classes
where grades are for improvement
   and your effort passes

much more than that
   your score would reach
to the higher range
   so you could teach

*that the lesson is
    the lesson you earn
from each experience
    you had to learn*

*a better thought
    to know and discern
what can't be taught
    so each gets their turn*

*to learn from mistakes
    and repeat them no more
to take a life course
    and get a good score*

*you are given chances
    to retake each test
move on to the next
    and forgive the rest*

*that is the way
    to be a success
and in the end you can say
    I did my best*

*(you will also be judged
    on the effort you made
but will be grading yourself
    on Graduation Day)*

[I see you just gave
  yourself a grade
the course isn't over
  there's still time for an 'A'

and I'll give you hints
  tell you what to say
love is the answer
  the rest of the way]

About the Author

Paul Gorman is an architect and poet
who grew up near the Baltimore homes
of Ogden Nash and Edgar Allen Poe.
He now resides in beautiful Frederick, Maryland,
that was home to Francis Scott Key
and John Greenleaf Whittier.

Previous works include: *Poems of Life, Love, and the Meaning of Meaning; Poet Gone Wild; and Sojourn.*

email contact: gormanpoetry@gmail.com

www.ingramcontent.com/pod-product-compliance
Lightning Source LLC
Chambersburg PA
CBHW030557080526
44585CB00012B/408